Upon a hill at the North Pole, under the dancing Aurora, Santa's workshop was buzzing with excitement. Christmas was drawing closer, and there was so much work to get done. Helper elves were rushing back and forth, stumbling over each other, hoping to finish all the presents in time for Christmas morning.

They wrapped with a swish,
taped with a snap,
stitched with a rhythm,
and snipped with a clap.

One elf, who was exhausted from working so hard, even fell
asleep on the job!

"Wake up, Holly-Jolly," shouted Zoomie. "You can sleep once all the kids are happy!" The tired elf looked up to see who had spoken, but Zoomie was already gone, so he yawned and slowly drifted back to sleep once more.

Santa flicked open his Good Kid Scroll — whoops! It sprang free, tumbling across the workshop floor and out the back door.

"Ho! Ho! Oh, no!" Santa chuckled. "That's a lot of good boys and girls this year!"

Sparkle's mouth popped open in surprise. "Golly, Santa! With so many, how will we ever finish on time?"

With a twinkle in his eye, Santa turned to his quickest and strongest elf.

"Zippie, to the forest, fast! We need a helping hand from our woodland friends," he said.

Zippie dashed back into the workshop later that evening. "The blizzard's been fierce, but we've got brave volunteers," he said, beaming as he introduced the shivering trio of hedgehogs, a pair of rabbits, and a determined frog.

Santa cheered, "That's wonderful!"

"And meeeeeeee," the Otter said as he jumped up and down behind Zippy, so Santa could see him. "I'm here to help too."

"Splendid! Every helper counts," said Santa, giving the group a big warm hug. "Ho Ho HOOO—OUCH!"

Santa shouted as a hedgehog's quill poked his big tummy. "Hehe, oops! My spikes can be a bit prickly," the hedgehog chuckled. "I'm not on the naughty list now, am I?" she said jokingly.
"Oh, not at all. It's a sign you're just the one for a very special job," Santa winked, already plotting the perfect task for her.

The hedgehogs were master painters, so they were assigned to the present production department. They dipped their quills in paint and rolled over the toys, creating beautiful colour patterns.

"Oh, darlings, those patterns are fabulous!" gushed Jay.

Meanwhile, the two rabbits helped pack the presents, their paws working at lightning speed.

"Look at that! I have never seen a present wrapped so fast and neatly," cheered Twinkle.
"You guys rock!" said Spike as he high-fived them.

As Sparkle was going on her break, she caught the frog grabbing peppermint drops with his tongue while no one was looking.

'Hey, we need those for Christmas!' she teased.
The frog blushed. 'Oops... ribbit!' he said, taking the sweet out of his mouth and placing it back where he found it. "Come with me," Sparkle continued. "Since you can jump higher than anyone else, I have the perfect job for you. I challenge you to clean as many cobwebs as you can from the factory ceiling by using those springy legs of yours".

"'YES" the frog replied eagerly. "I'll be done in a flash—watch this!" he said determinedly. He bent his legs... BOING.

With a knowing smile, Mrs Claus looked at the tired faces around her. She turned to the otter. "Come along, dear, I have just the thing to give every elf and creature a big boost of energy. But shhh, it's a Claus family secret recipe. With your helping paws, we'll be done in a jiffy."

The otter wagged his tail, excited to help, and scampered along beside her to the kitchen.

The otter was quite the little rascal, pinching pieces of cookie dough when he thought Mrs. Claus wasn't looking.

Tray after tray was filled with scrumptious, chocolate-dipped shortbread cookies, but some had mysteriously disappeared. "Hmm," Mrs. Claus pondered with a playful glance at the trays, "I'm sure we had more cookies than this..."

"Time for a snack, my busy helpers!" Mrs. Claus's voice rang out warmly as she gracefully entered the workshop, with the otter waddling proudly beside her, his tiny paws holding a stack of cookies that filled the room with a buttery, sweet smell. The elves and woodland creatures clapped and cheered. The frog zapped a cookie with his quick tongue. "Yum-yum! What a treat!" he cheered with a hop. "You're the best, Mrs. Claus!"

Mrs. Claus thanked the otter by giving him a red bag of beans—wrapped with a golden ribbon—that she had grown in her greenhouse.

"Santa! Santa! SANTA!" the otter blurted out, so full of energy from all the cookies he had eaten. "I just finished helping Mrs. Claus! Anything else I can do?" Santa looked at the little ball of jumping fur, who was still licking the chocolate off his lips. He paused and stroked his beard in thought. "AHA," he said, "I have just the job for all that energy. Come, follow me."

As they walked, Santa asked, "What is your name again, my friend?" The otter replied, "My name's Tooter, Santa." Tooter opened the bag and saw it was full of colourful beans. He took one and ate it. It tasted like a rainbow on a crisp winter morning, bursting with delicious flavour!

"Tooter?" Santa raised an eyebrow playfully. "That's an unusual name indeed." Just then, Tooter's tummy rumbled... louder and louder until he let out a big, thunderous fart. "Oh ho ho ho," Santa laughed so hard, his big belly wobbling like a bowl of jelly. "I understand now. Well, Tooter, that's a name with a story to tell!"

"Yup, you got that right; I have so many to tell you. This one time, I was building a treehouse and I—"

Huuuuh," Santa suddenly gasped.

Tooter looked at Santa, his eyes wide with alarm. "What's wrong, Santa?" Tooter asked. "It's the reindeer, look closely at them," replied Santa.

Tooter looked over at the reindeer and saw something odd – they were perfectly still, snuggled up in their hay beds, sleeping so soundly that you could see their bellies gently moving up and down. There was no twinkling magic around them. Usually, each reindeer had a gentle glow, a sign of their magical power to fly high in the sky. But now, that special sparkle was missing. Even Rudolph's red nose, normally as bright as a shining star, was fading away.

Santa knelt beside them, whispering, "What's the matter, my dear friends?" He patted each one gently, feeling their foreheads. "Let's get up, Donner," he said softly, but Donner just twitched his ear, remaining fast asleep. He nudged Blitzen, who snorted quietly, his warm breath fogging in the chilly air. Vixen's nose gave a little twitch, and Comet's hooves moved slightly, but there was no sign of their usual sparkling energy. Santa, filled with concern, muttered, "It's unlike you all to be so silent."

"Tooter," he said softly, "if our reindeer friends can't fly tonight, we won't be able to deliver the gifts. It's hard to imagine so many children waking up on Christmas morning without any presents. It's our job to make sure every child wakes up to a day filled with joy and surprise. We all worked so hard to make Christmas special. What if it won't happen at all?"

"We can't let that happen, Santa. There's got to be something we can do!" said Tooter. Santa placed a reassuring hand on the young otter's shoulder, grateful for his unwavering spirit. "You're right, Tooter. Your faith in the magic of Christmas is exactly what we need at this moment. Let's think. Together, we can surely find a solution."

"Hmmm... I wonder if they might just be hungry. I know that when I'm hungry, I don't feel like myself either." With a little nod, he dug his furry paw into the red bag and pulled out a handful of shiny, yummy beans. He tiptoed over to each reindeer and carefully tucked a bean into their mouths, being as gentle as a snowflake landing on the ground. Santa, puzzled, asked, "Why the beans, Tooter?" Tooter smiled and said, "A little snack cheers me up, so I thought it might work for them too!" Santa gave a soft laugh. He was so thankful that Tooter was trying his best.

A few moments later, the reindeers' tummies rumbled; the rumbling was getting louder and louder, then...

PFFFFFFFFT
THRRRRRRP
BRAP BRAP BRAP

One by one, the reindeer tooted, unable to stop. It was like a musical chorus of farts. The more they did, the lighter they got, and soon, each reindeer began to float. Their magic had returned... only a little stinkier than before!

"Tooter, you're a hero! You brought back their magic!" Santa cheered as he gave Tooter a massive hug and spun him around and around. "Haha, Santa, be careful, I ate so many cookies and beans, I might throw up," Tooter giggled. After the hug, Tooter looked up with wide, curious eyes. "But Santa, how did the magic come back?"

Santa knelt down, his eyes twinkling. "Their magic, Tooter, like all the magic here in the North Pole, comes from love and friendship. When you shared your snacks and were kind, you helped their magic shine again! And the... unique power of Mrs. Claus's beans added just the right spark!"

DING DONG,
the old grandfather clock chimed.

"Ho Ho Ho, look at the time! We really must hurry!" With excitement, Tooter hopped onto Santa's back, and they hurried to the workshop to get ready for the big night.

"Load the presents!" Santa boomed. The elves and their woodland friends hustled, their footsteps a soft patter against the floor. Presents thudded gently into the sleigh, each landing with a muffled thump. "Heave-ho!" the elves chorused, carefully arranging the colourful parcels.

At last, the sleigh was ready. Santa turned to Tooter and asked with a smile, "Tooter, would you do me the honour of accompanying me tonight?"

Tooter's eyes lit up with excitement. "Wow, Santa, really? I'd love to help deliver gifts to all the good boys and girls!" he exclaimed, bouncing up and down.

But then, as he hopped, he had a sudden thought and stopped. He realised the sleigh would go high up into the clouds, and his feet wouldn't be able to touch the ground anymore. Looking down at his feet, he worried about what Santa and all the elves and creatures around would say. "But... but Santa, I'm scared of heights," he confessed. "The thought of being up so high makes my tail shake."

"You can do it, Tooter!" shouted Twinkle.

"You've got this, dude! Go rock those heights!" Spike said, giving the otter a fist pump in the air.

As loud as he could, Jay yelled, "Go for it, darling! Be fearless, fabulous, and fly high!"

"Zoom through the skies, Tooter! Just like racing in my chair, going fast is a blast – you're going to love it!" Zoomie said as she twirled around.

The frog leaped up high, his voice shouting, "TOOTER!"… BOING, "TOOTER!"… BOING, "TOOTER!"… BOING, with each enthusiastic jump.

The hedgehog trio chimed in: "TOOTER!" "TOOTER!" "TOOTER!"

One by one, the elves and woodland creatures started rooting for the little otter, and before you knew it, the entire North Pole team was clapping and cheering for Tooter as loud as they could.

The support from his friends, old and new, echoed around him, and he looked on as they waved their hands - some webbed, some not - along with claws and paws, in encouragement. He felt his insides go warm and fuzzy, and tears welled up in his eyes.

He saw how much his friends believed in him, and he started to believe in himself more. "I see what you mean, Santa... kindness and love really do help you feel magical. I am still nervous, but I want to try my best and do it anyway, for everyone here, for every child waiting for Christmas - I want to make them all proud!"

Tooter climbed into the sleigh behind Santa, took a deep breath, and steadied himself. Looking up at the sky with determination, he grabbed onto Santa's hand tightly. "You know, Tooter," said Santa, "being brave isn't about not being scared at all. It's about being scared but still trying to do it anyway, and we are all so proud of your bravery."

He smiled gently at Tooter, adding in a whisper, "Here's a secret - I have fears too. Like balloons! They can pop so unexpectedly, it startles me every time. But each year, I blow them up for Mrs. Claus's birthday. It's the small acts of courage that count."

"I guess... everyone has fears, and that's okay, because friends and family will always help you through it," Tooter replied.

"Let's do this," Tooter said, his face breaking into a huge smile. "In 3... 2... 1... Toots away!"
Tooter and Santa pulled on the reins, giving the 12 reindeer their cue. At the same time,
they let out a symphony of farts –

"PFFFFT! BRAPP! BRRRRRT! SQUEAK! BLARP BLARP BLARP!"

–and the sleigh shot forward into the air at record speed, sending a cloud of stinky toot
gas at Santa and Tooter. "This will be the merriest, stinkiest Christmas ever," Santa joked,
pinching his nose with a clothespin. He gave one to Tooter, who politely declined. "I don't
really mind the smell," he said. Santa laughed and replied, "I should have guessed!"

Up in the sky, Tooter looked down. "Wow!" he gasped. Below them, the snowy ground sparkled like glitter. The cold air made soft whooshing sounds, making Tooter feel like a superhero.

"See that, Tooter?" Santa pointed at the colourful Northern Lights. They were dancing in the sky like a rainbow! They flew over tall, icy mountains and shiny frozen lakes. The trees below looked like a giant's snowy garden. The reindeer flew smoothly, their antlers twinkling like stars. Tooter's eyes grew wide. This was the most magical ride ever! "Santa, it's so pretty!" Tooter cheered. Santa laughed. "That's the Christmas magic, Tooter. You're a part of it now!" Tooter realised he wasn't as scared anymore. Looking at the world from so high was so much fun!

Santa and Tooter were flying all night. The reindeer tried so hard to be quiet with their toots. They made funny faces and went, "Pfft!" very softly. But as the sky started to get bright, the sleigh began to slow down. "Uh-oh," said Santa, "Looks like our reindeer are out of toot power!"

"Oh no, we're slowing down!" Santa said, a bit worried. "How will we get home?" But Tooter had a plan. He opened the bag of beans. There were only five beans left — not enough for all twelve reindeer, but... "Don't worry, Santa," he said. "I've got this!" And then, munch, munch, munch, he ate all five toot beans.

Tooter stood and held onto Santa as a massive, rumbling toot exploded from his tushy. 'Toots awayyyyyy!' he cried out joyfully. The sleigh took off like a fart rocket! Santa laughed heartily, holding the reins tightly as his hat sailed off into the wind. "Ho, ho, oh no! My hat!" he chuckled. "Well, maybe a lucky child will find it in the morning. What a special Christmas surprise that would be!"

"How did you make it back so quickly?" Mrs. Claus asked when they returned in record time. "And where's your hat?"

"Ho, ho, ho, never mind about that," Santa chuckled. "I will fill you in later, but for now... I think it's time to celebrate!"

Laughter and dance lit up the frosty night,
Tooter's toots rang out, a true delight.
Santa clapped and laughed, leading the way,
Mrs. Claus twirled around, so gracefully

Zoomie did a spin, sparkling like a star,
Froggy's jumps were big, he leaped so far.
Spike's electric guitar roared like a bear,
While the rabbits clapped to the beat, a perfect pair.

Hedgehogs giggled, rolled and shouted "Yippeeee"
As Zippy juggled them, so merrily
Sparkle, Twinkle, and Jay, danced without a care,
Faces all smiling, joy they did share.

Santa raised his glass, his eyes full of cheer,
"To Tooter, our hero, who conquered his fear.
With his mighty farts, he saved the day,
Bringing joy and laughter in a wonderful way!"

Tooter blushed and smiled, his heart aglow,
then he spoke warmly, letting his feelings flow
"Thanks to you, dear friends, so true,
with your love and help, we made Christmas come through"

We did it all, in our own unique way
So cheers to us, hip hip hooray
Let's say it all together

Toots awayyyyyy!

Mrs Claus's Secret Cookie Recipe

Ingredients:

2 cups all-purpose flour
1/4 teaspoon salt
1 cup unsalted butter, softened
1/2 cup powdered sugar
1 teaspoon vanilla extract
2 cups chocolate chips (semi-sweet or dark)
Sprinkles, crushed candy canes, or mini marshmallows for topping
Optional: 1/4 teaspoon peppermint extract for a holiday twist

Making the Cookie Dough

Warm-Up the Oven: First things first, let's wake up the oven! Set it to 350°F (that's 175°C). Then, take a baking sheet and cover it with parchment paper so the cookies won't stick.

Mixing Flour and Salt: In a big bowl, let's mix our magic dust – the flour and salt. Whisk them together like you're a wizard!

Butter and Sugar Fun: In another bowl, let's take the soft butter and powdered sugar and mix them until they look fluffy like a cloud.

Vanilla and Peppermint Magic
Now, let's add the vanilla extract to our fluffy mix.
If you want it to taste like Christmas, add a tiny bit of peppermint extract too!

Creating the Dough

It's time to slowly add our magic dust (the flour and salt mix) to the buttery cloud.
Keep mixing until it looks like cookie dough - soft and smooth.

Shaping Our Cookies

Rolling the Dough: Sprinkle some flour on a clean surface and
roll the dough until it's as thick as a pencil.

Cutting Shapes

Use your favourite cookie cutters - stars, snowflakes, or trees -
and press them into the dough to make nice shapes.

Baking Time

Carefully place your cookie shapes on the baking sheet. Let's bake them in the oven for 12-15 minutes.
You'll know they're ready when the edges are just a bit golden.

Cooling Down

After baking, let them sit on a wire rack.

Chocolate Dipping Time

Melting Chocolate: Put the chocolate chips in a microwave-safe bowl.
Heat them for 20 seconds, then stir, and repeat until the chocolate is all melty and smooth.

Decorating Our Cookies

Dipping in Chocolate: Dip half of each cookie into the melted chocolate.
It's like giving the cookies a chocolate blanket!

Adding Toppings

Now, sprinkle your cookies with fun stuff like sprinkles, candy cane pieces, or mini marshmallows.
Make them look like they're ready for a party!

The Final Touch

Let the Chocolate Set. Place your decorated cookies back on the parchment paper.
The chocolate needs to harden. If you're in a hurry, pop them in the fridge for 15 minutes.

And there you have it! Your very own, super special,
Chocolate-Dipped Shortbread Cookies! Great job, Chef!

Visit my instagram
@ChangeTheWorldWithKaryn

For some fun colouring pages of Tooter and the gang

Hello, beautiful people! I truly hope you've had an absolutely Toot-TASTIC journey through the pages of this book. As my debut in the realm of children's literature, I can't express enough how joyous and nostalgic it was for me to create this story. It's a reflection of the laughter-filled childhood I cherished, full of jokes and fun times with my family that continue to brighten our days. My wish is that this tale has sprinkled a little extra sparkle on your Christmas, igniting inspiration and creating joyful memories for you and your little ones.

The magic of a wonderful childhood and the gift of education are beliefs I hold dear. This is why I'm dedicating 20% of my proceeds to support educational initiatives at Cansumbol Elementary School, a place very close to my heart as my mother's alma mater. She, along with my father, has been a pillar of resilience and strength in my life.

Embarking on the journey of creating my first children's book was an eye-opener to the dedication and work it entails. A little note to myself: don't underestimate the time it takes!... and NEVER start a children's Christmas book in October!

I'm immensely grateful for my fantastic team, whose talent and passion were instrumental in bringing this project to life. Just like Santa in our story who relied on his friends to prepare for Christmas, I too found invaluable support in my team. A heartfelt thank you to...

Fábio Luis Ribeiro is from Brazil and has been an Illustrator for 15 years. He is Deeply passionate about art and bringing great stories to life

Sanika Desai is an illustrator and designer born in India. She studied accessory design but has always been passionate about storytelling through illustrations. She started her journey as an illustrator soon after graduation and has worked on a range of projects.

Ivan is a 45 year old Brazilian who works as a public servant in the city of Araxá in Minas Gerais. He is a talented writer and cartoonist.

Made in the USA
Las Vegas, NV
19 December 2023

83173835R00029